The Desiderata
of Faith

The Desiderata
of Faith

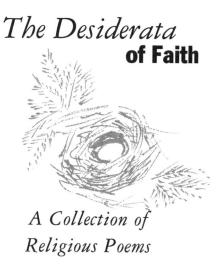

A Collection of
Religious Poems

Max Ehrmann

Illustrations by Sally Sturman

Crown Publishers, Inc.
New York

Published by Crown Publishers, Inc., 201 East 50th Street,
New York, New York 10022. Member of the
Crown Publishing Group.

Random House, Inc. New York, Toronto, London, Sydney, Auckland

CROWN is a trademark of Crown Publishers, Inc.

Manufactured in the United States of America

Book design by Linda Kocur with Nancy Kenmore

Library of Congress Cataloging-in-Publication Data
Ehrmann, Max, 1872-1945.
The desiderata of faith: a collection of religious poems/
Max Ehrmann.— 1st ed.
1. Religious poetry, American. I. Title.
PS3509. H7D39   1996
811'.52—dc20   95-22771
CIP

ISBN 0-517-70331-9

10 9 8 7 6 5 4 3 2 1

First Edition

contents

introduction

Long I pondered as I attempted to write this introduction. Should it be of the innocence of childhood, or perhaps the daily grind of work as an adult? Or perhaps the more contemplative thoughts of retirement and old age?

To some, God does not exist.

To many, God is an avenger, who will cast poor sinners into a burning hell for their transgressions.

For most, God is loving, and will forgive mankind's sins.

It is a rare person indeed, who in a crisis, does not mutter an involuntary prayer for help or comfort from the terror and despair that surrounds.

Read Max Ehrmann's thoughts in "Thou Whom We Call God," and see how they fit so neatly the confusion of the late 20th century—

Long has been the time since I spoke with Thee, Thou

whom we call God. . . .

Come Thou near me, as in olden days when I saw

Thee everywhere . . .

This prayer is born of my need . . .

Many know Max Ehrmann only through his great work *Desiderata*. With this book, you will see his perception of mankind's problems, and the depth of his power.

Robert L. Bell

8

The Desiderata
of Faith

desiderata

Go placidly amid the noise and haste, and
remember what peace there may be in silence.
As far as possible, without surrender, be on good
terms with all persons. Speak your truth quietly and
clearly; and listen to others, even to the dull and
ignorant; they too have their story. Avoid loud
and aggressive persons; they are vexatious to the
spirit. If you compare yourself with others, you
may become vain or bitter, for always there will be
greater and lesser persons than yourself. Enjoy
your achievements as well as your plans. Keep
interested in your own career, however humble; it is
a real possession in the changing fortunes of time.
Exercise caution in your business affairs, for the
world is full of trickery. But let this not blind you to
what virtue there is; many persons strive for high
ideals, and everywhere life is full of heroism. Be

yourself. Especially do not feign affection. Neither be cynical about love; for in the face of all aridity and disenchantment, it is as perennial as the grass. Take kindly the counsel of the years, gracefully surrendering the things of youth. Nurture strength of spirit to shield you in sudden misfortune. But do not distress yourself with dark imaginings. Many fears are born of fatigue and loneliness. Beyond a wholesome discipline, be gentle with yourself. You are a child of the universe no less than the trees and the stars; you have a right to be here. And whether or not it is clear to you, no doubt the universe is unfolding as it should. Therefore be at peace with God, whatever you concieve Him to be. And whatever your labors and aspirations, in the noisy confusion of life, keep peace in your soul. With all its sham, drudgery and broken dreams, it is still a beautiful world. Be cheerful. Strive to be happy.

thou whom we **call God!**

Long has been the time since I spoke with Thee,
Thou whom we call God. Now I soften the stern
face I carry upon the street as a weapon in the
struggle for existence, and I cast out of myself the
evil of the world, all possession, all malice;
and I yield up my soul, as a flower lifts its petals
in the twilight of morning.

Unbind me from the things of the earth, and
let me wander through the world like the still stars
of the night. Come Thou near me, as in olden days
when I saw Thee everywhere, in the woods and
the sky, and heard Thy voice in the silence of the
fields. Take my hand and lead me as my earthly
father when my steps were feeble. Teach me again
to love, and make soft my voice with gentle words.

12

As a gardener waters his garden, refresh Thou my soul with tenderness, and bring peace within the troubled household of my heart. Knock at my door in the lonesome night; and as I have need of Thee, send me forth to others who sit with drooping faces at the table of despair and see Thee not.

This prayer is born of my need; and if indeed men convince me that Thou are not, and that these words are spoken but to die unheard, yet have I been answered, and shall believe that Thou art— Thou whom we call God!

the voice

I sought to write a lofty theme,
Some sweet and righteous poet's dream;
When quick there came from out my heart
A ghastly voice that made me start:
"Such work is for the just," it said,
"Almost thy heart and soul are dead;
If thou would'st lead men to the light,
First bring thyself from out the night."

autumn

Now the great green earth has turned to gold;
and the fruit is gathered, and the grain is garnered.

So may we in the autumn of life, mellowed by
experience, grow rich in beauty and service, as the
green of the earth and the grain of the field.

where **God is**

"God's in his world and all is well,"

Said the man who had stores of worldly things.

"There is no God and the world is hell,"

Said the man who had need of worldly things.

For life needs rest

Before it is blest

By the God that we say is good,

And the pain of toil

Will surely spoil

The faith that had understood

Our God to be naught but just.

So let's bring rest

To the wearied breast

And not let goodness rust,

For love's a thing

That God will bring,

And God is one who thrives the best

Not in pain from o'er toil where poverty dwells,

But where there's work's reward and rest—

That's the place where our God most often dwells.

who entereth
here
(for the door of your dream house)

Whoe'er thou art that entereth here,
  Forget the struggling world
And every trembling fear.

Take from thy heart each evil thought,
  And all that selfishness
Within thy life hath wrought.

For once inside this place thou'lt find
  No barter, servant's fear,
Nor master's voice unkind.

Here all are kin of God above—
  Thou, too, dear heart; and here
The rule of life is love.

16

journey's
end

Have we learned wisdom in the great book of life, that we may have repose in age? Then let us not fear, that we may sit without discontent in the house of our narrow wanderings. Let us be patient with youth remembering that its joys and follies were ours also in cheerful yesterdays. When weariness overtakes us, may courage and gentleness forsake us not. When we despair in darkness, may we see a light before our faltering footsteps.

Now are we thankful for our lives and for the abundance of the earth, for the moon and the stars, the sunshine and the rain, the fields and the woods. Above all, we are thankful for love.

And at journey's end, the sun gone down, let us walk with smiling faces like travelers homeward bound.

an artist's
prayer

Lord God, thou who dost paint with magic touch
The curtains of the soft and silent night,
This gift I ask, that o'er whatever cloth
My brush may glide, now to and fro and 'round,
There will come that which ever pleases thee.
Help me to make the things that beauty hold
Amid these veering lines and diverse shades,
That cheer will bring to sad and solemn men
And tired women in their dreary haunts,
That youth will not forget on highways hard
With troubled years, when somber night is on,
And when no kindly light leads through the way,
That joy and love may dawn like newborn days
In hearts where long the chambers have been dark.
Let lowly life and dusty daily toil
Come near me evermore and day by day,

That I forget not them that still are kind
Though tried by years of unrequited toil,
Alas! and sometimes want and age and pain.
Let me not love my pictures more than men,
Nor follow the wild lead of some mad dream,
Nor see myself as if above the crowd
Commanding that they all shall bow their heads;
Instead, with kindly heart and gentle hand
And smiles upon my face, let me serve them
Whose muscles ache at evening's twilight fall
While mine in comfort still are fresh and strong.
May all these be not empty, idle words,
But all the burden of my life's sweet task.
And when thou seest that my work is done,
Let me feel thy soft evening shadows fall
As when I climbed into my nursery bed
With childish faith in time's old long ago;
And let the kiss of peace lie on my lips.

revelation

I.

Once, after long weeks in the dust and heat
    of the city—
        in the noisy strife of the crowded world—
        covered daily with the grime of toil—
Once, I say, I stood in the still night upon
    the shore of a lake; and for a long time
    I watched the lurid west.
And with my own eyes I saw God painting upon
    the sky-curtain of the softening dark;
And, after a while, the moon and her brood
    of stars wandered through the night;
And I said to myself I need no bibles
    of old revelation;
        this is revelation; out of this beauty
        is my faith born.

II.

Now that night is passed, and I again hear the noise
and feel the grime of the crowded world;
But now I am more patient and longer suffering,
for all I know that
nightly God is painting His revelation on the sky-
curtain over the lake where I stood.
And over every lake, and over the crest of every
hill, and over the green level of every open field,
and if we could but see, over the
sky-obscuring houses of every city—
is God painting His revelation.

to the masters **of men**

They that toil—
What have done that they should beg
To work and run by your command?
I cannot understand.

They that toil—
Why do they fear some heartless ill
When you draw near their slavish life,
Bound to unending strife?

They that toil—
Some day they'll know this earth is for
Them too, and lo! who shall withstand
Their loud and fierce command?

They that toil—
They slumber now; but they shall wake
And they shall know their mighty power
In that strange reckoning hour.

They that toil—
God made them, too, with love of life
No less than you—in breaking storms
They'll come in myriad swarms.

Therefore, O
Ye masters all! ere whirlwinds rise
And temples fall, and daylight wane,
On earth let justice reign!

progressive
confessional

Asceticism.

I have known earthly joys, and yet
In byways oft at night I've met,
As years have moved so swiftly on,
Some secret pain from out the past
That had its birth in pleasures gone
And made me beg God's grace at last.

Scepticism.

And yet so many deeds called wrong
Have brought me joys in goodly throng;
And many deeds that men call good
Have plunged me in the deepest dark;
I doubt that e'er I understood
On which God puts his righteous mark.

Positivism.

Now this one thing is clear to me;
That laws, howe'er proclaimed to be
From God, if they 'gainst nature go,
Are human made, and do confess
Man's ignorance. For this I know,
Our God has meant us happiness.

an easter

prayer

Resurrect Thou the dreams and songs and love
　　that enchanted the garden of my youth, filled
　　with joys of a thousand hopes in the still
　　morning's twilight, and dawning visions in the
　　shadowed, starry night. As the kindly earth
　　yields forth each spring her budding brood, so
　　in the barren winter of my heart may there bloom
　　again the rose of sweet content.

O'er the din of the world and the strife of men, let
　　rise the symphonies of eternal peace. Resurrect
　　them that slumber in graves of gold; and deliver
　　humanity from those cruel conventions that are
　　but the husks of virtue. Make kindness king,
　　and teach us that good deeds are greater than
　　philosophy. To tired men that daily tread
　　the crowded streets, give Thou a place of sweet

repose at night; and fill with love the hearts of
lonely women. Bring forth sweet babes
from out the arms of each, to light with joy the
byways of the earth.

Thou Great God, uphold me also in the lonely hour;
    and though I fall in the din and the dust
    of the world, resurrect Thou me. Even to the last,
    turn my hands to kindly service, and part my lips
    in gleeful songs of love. And in the softly falling
    dark, when all grows strangely still, may I be
    glad to have trod the sweet green earth, and
    know the tender touch of love. Yet may I depart
    with joy, as one who journeys home at evening.

the beloved **dead**

How peaceful lie the dead! Why do we weep, since they mourn not? Well-beaten is the path they take into the great unknown. We follow them a little way, till dusk to darkness turns, then parting wave farewell. We do not know what waits their journey's end, but as we trust the sun will rise each morn, so we trust that the mystery of life and death one day will be explained, and we shall be content.

Farewell, thou gentle sleeper—perhaps not forever; soon we too shall pass out of the beautiful earth. In faith's bright hours, the ever-dawning, deathless hope of all the ages tells us that somehow we shall know thee again. We speak in earthly symbols; we know not the language of the country beyond life. Art thou already seated near the helmsman of the universe, in wonder cruising some celestial sea of worlds? Dost thou with kindly memory still look upon our little earth? And wilt thou sometimes think of us, remembering happy hours we spent together in this radiant sun-kissed world?

Thus shall we not be all alone; for often thou wilt come to us and we shall see thee by our side, and in the stillness hear thy voice. Speak to us in spirit whispers, when sorrow bears us down! Thy placid face now tells us not to grieve, for peace is thine.

Farewell, thou gentle sleeper. How still thou art!

God

Somewhere, once, I expressed a belief in the
certainty of God. And I was challenged to tell what
God is. But I could not. Much less could I tell what
he is than an insect could tell what I am. But there
is something in this universe which is more than
we—Oh, very much more than we—painter,
architect, inventor, consummate genius, who built
the house of the universe, and overlaid it with
emerald, gold, and sapphire and garnished the dome
with the star-tapestry of the night; who planned the
course of the sun, and of the moon; and built the
iris temples of the sunset clouds; and planted
the longing for love in the heart of the world; and
made the sea and the moan of the sea; and made the
laws of his house honest, unchanging laws, for man
to learn and labor by, in gladness and peace. And
this is something more than we—oh, very much
more than we—surely this is God!

ships returning **home**

We all are ships returning home laden with life's experience, memories of work, good times and sorrows, each with his special cargo;

And it is our common lot to show the marks of the voyage, here a shattered prow, there a patched rigging, and every hulk turned black by the unceasing batter of the restless wave.

May we be thankful for fair weather and smooth seas, and in times of storm have the courage and patience that mark every good mariner;

And, over all, may we have the cheering hope of joyful meetings, as our ship at last drops anchor in the still water of the eternal harbor.

31

ego

ipse

All the questions have I asked,
All things have I tried;
But nothing satisfied.
"There is no vital task
Except to wait till time has fled
And I am dead,"
I said.

Thus I walked in living death,
Smiled at God's great trick
Of life, till I grew sick
Of smiles; and then in breath
All hot and vile with bitter cry
I prayed that I
Might die.

Back I pushed all human creeds,
Standing lone and nude
With God in solitude,
And lo! from out the weeds
Of human thought I looked in awe,
MYSELF I saw
Was law.

faith

When I remember all the years,
How full of love my heart hath been,
To drive out darkness, dry up tears,
And bid sweet faith come in . . .

Now oft I sit, when night's o'erspread,
With unread book upon my knee,
Waiting, listening for some dear tread
To bring back faith to me.

prayer
for repose

When I observe how most men rise to power;
Inheritance, industrious selfishness,
Unceasing nerve-exhausting strain and stress,
Some gifts from cross-eyed fortune's lucky hour,
Spectacular effects from which may flower
The ballyhoo of radio and press—
When I observe how most men reach success,
I have no wish to scale this giddy tower.

Dear God, when will there come the quiet voice,
The gentle manner and the placid tread,
Content to be unselfish men, the choice
Not singly but together forge ahead?
Our time is short. Before we close
The book of life, give us to know repose.

the last
prayer

I am weary lying here so long. Many things that once I thought important do not seem so now. If this is the end of earth for me, I pray I shall have a last conscious moment in which I may gladly remember that, in the days of my strength, I had the courage now and then to raise my voice for the right as I saw it; that amid the struggles for the necessities of existence I had time to record a few moments of spiritual ecstasy; and that in the stern ways of life I had known the tenderness of a woman's love. May these things abide with me; and if in the infinite universe I retain aught of my earthly self, may they remind me that in my feeble way I was one who tried—a lovely memory out of the beautiful earth. Then closing my eyes—consciousness slowly dwindling like a day that is spent—let me fall quietly asleep, a tired child at sundown. Peace.

prayer
in war time

Star charmed, we have dreamed of peaceful ages;
Dreamed of mighty empires ruled by tenderness.
O Lord, whose cunning fingers weave the night,
And hang the sky with jeweled tapestry,
Make good the whispers of the myriad stars,
Unbroken keep the promise of the moon,
That love, not might, shall be the law of life!
This awful paradox, O Lord, give us
To know: That we must kill that love may live!

a
psalm

When I wander in places of greed for gain I have no desire; the grass of the meadow and the stars of the night comfort me. Though darkness overcome me, I shall not despair; the God of my youth still abides with me. He showeth me the palaces of the rich and the haunts of the poor, yet keepeth sweet my soul. When weariness overtakes me, I lie down in slumber, and the peace of the world is upon me. Though poverty abide with me, I pray that courage and gentleness forsake me not. And with all living things out of the earth and out of other worlds I believe I shall grow in the fields of God forever.

i went into a magnificent
church

I went into a magnificent church in a great city, and I heard the minister tell the people about Christ.

And the longer I listened the more I wondered why the people did not silence him.

For, as I looked around me, I saw them that had crucified Christ, and them that defamed Him and turned Him out.

And when I left the church, I went without the city to a wood; and there I sat for a long time thinking of the sweet-souled Christs that had yet to die that love might some day flourish on the earth.

And I remembered how dearly liberty had been bought from the self-righteous masters of each age, who worshipped according to the fashion; and my thoughts were somehow heavy with the sorrow of the world.

There in the whispering wood, where every leaf was a tongue softly humming the songs of summer, the beauty of the world soon lifted me out of the things of the present, like a melody remembered out of childhood; and there I, too, silently within, prayed that I might at least once in my life boldly strike the iron harpstrings of the heroic.

And soon darkness came on, and the lights of the city looked out into the night; and on my way back, as I went by the magnificent church, it was silent and dark; yet I somehow fancied that I could still hear the minister telling the people about Christ.

As I turned away from the great stone arches of the magnificent church, now sullenly grand in the mystic glimmer of the night, I remembered that the Son of Man wandered barefoot over the Judean hills, and at night had nowhere to lay His head.

thou that art **idle born**

Thou that art idle born—

    knowest thou thy weariness of toil

    When the flesh refuses and cries "no farther,"

    And the soul believes no longer in God,

    And the night and the day are hateful;

    When fear of want knocks ever at the door.

    And evil dreams harass thy midnight sleep?

There are none such, sayest thou?

    They are in thy house, in the street, everywhere.

    They adore thee, thy imperious manner,

    Thy placid eyes, and thy careless self-assurance,

    Thy soft white flesh—

    Thou—thou that art idle born!

What great virtue is thine
    That God has so elevated thee
    That men and women and children serve thee,

    Yet thou servest not at all?
    And what great wrong have they done
    Who serve always yet are never served?
    Does not God love them also?

oh,
lift us up!

Enamored with the lure of gilded show,
Our hearts are palsied and our souls lie low.
We have gone blind in search of sordid things;
The groveling strain of life has clipped our wings.

Oh, lift us up in soul, and lift our eyes,
That we behold the jewel embedded skies,
And find again content in sunlit scenes
Of quiet woods and windswept meadow greens.

Renew the sweetness of the bloom of youth,
The love of simple things, the love of truth.
With beauty didst thou fill the earth's great cup;
Thou God of all the world, Oh, lift us up!

dark **days**

What fool shall say, "My days are fair,
God's in his world and all is well,"
When half mankind shrieks in despair
Worse than in Dante's flaming hell!

I cannot sing in happy mood
While hostile armies take their toll.
On these dark days I toil and brood
With starless midnight in my soul.

And yet, O World, O Life, O God!
I find myself, just as the fool,
Believing in thy chastening rod,
Believing still that love must rule.

certainty

Behold the night! The little gold ships sailing through the seas of the sky. They are the lighted candles in the house of the world. You and I also are a part of this glorified house of the world, lighted nightly by these million lamps.

Behold the sun flooding the earth with the liquid silver of dawn, and nursing tenderly each blade of grass and warming each head of grain, and going down at night amid the crimson and amber mountains of the sky.

What are old fables and the babble of philosophers compared to this wonder? Verily here is a miracle, and the tongue of man is dumb to speak its beauty.

Consider the love of the world—how men have nursed the dream of a better and gentler earth, and gone down in agony to death that justice might live and the downtrodden be lifted up! Surely these are the sons of God.

And consider the love of a man and a woman—how each finds an earthly paradise in the love of the other, and the world is born anew in tenderness and made to glow with strange beauty!

Consider man, noble in body, and greater than the sun, for the sun does not think.

To the question, "What is this thought-illuminated house of life?" We have no answer.

Verily here is the miracle of miracles! Out of the mystery and beauty of the world is born the dream of hope and the certainty of God.

I go forth to my labor and have no fear, for He that lighted the night with stars, and planted the forests, and made the grass to grow, will not deny me a place to labor in.

Each day I marvel anew at the Architect who built this house of the Universe,

I cannot tell you how little distraught I am about God and religion.

death and **life**

One does not like to think of death.

The summer, the grass, trees, friends, familiar
places—one likes to think of life!

Yet nearly all things in the world are lifeless things:
the earth, mountains, stone, rivers, iron, buildings,
etc., infinitely.

Nearly everything in the world is silent, as death is
silent, without love or grief or thought of anything.

All are chemicals, as my body is chemical, which
one day will return to its silent brotherhood of
chemicals.

But life—with its dreams and hates and loves and far-off mystic wanderings—what is life?

Why do not the mountains speak, and the stones love and grieve?

We can understand something of lifeless things, as death is lifeless.

Though living, we can not understand life.

May we learn to think not unkindly of death. If it has nothing else, it has what we living crave but may not have—peace, rest.

the light of a cheerful **heart**

I tell you that you and I and the commonest person are all journeying in the same way, hemmed in by the same narrow path, leading to the eternal years.

We pride ourselves over our particular superiority; but really there is little difference between us;

And in this journey over the thousand hills and valleys called life, he is wisest who is patient where the way is hard, has faith when he does not understand, and carries into the dark places the light of a cheerful heart.

parable

of the ship and the sea

Brother, why do we contend and injure one another?

We all are here together on this ship, that tosses about in an apparently limitless sea. Isolated in dark and silent waters, the ship appears to be voyaging somewhere. We do not know where the ship came from; but we know a little of its recent voyagings.

We know nothing of what port, if any, the ship is making for. We are huddled here together, some below, some on the decks. We see lights dotting the sea.

But none of us ever has seen another ship of people, of whom we might ask questions, such as, where their ship had been, and what they had learned of the sea, and if there were shores—perhaps beautiful shores— or if the sea was all that there is.

Lonely, mysteriously, our ship moves on. Does it know where it is going? Is there somewhere a pilot? Are there other ships going to a common port? We are lonely in the vast sea.

Brother, why do we contend and injure one another?

old
age

I know that this is not my native land.
All round me here
So much there is I do not understand,
Ofttimes I fear
And feel my way with outstretched hand.

Time was I fancied only pleasure real.
In careless youth
My dancing feet spun like a whirling wheel;
But now, in truth,
With cautious steps my way I feel.

I try to pierce the silent mystery round
Life's little day;
But in reply my calling brings no sound.
Along the way
The stones my bleeding footsoles wound.

Philosophies that babble of life's aim,

No solace bring.

I often searched but to no answer came.

What is this thing,

Man's learning, but a dim-lit flame!

My summons comes, I hope I shall not grieve,

Nor to and fro

Be tossed about in anguish at my leave.

But may I go

As one who wanders home at eve.

to be **loved**

To be loved in life is life's greatest gift.

To be loved in death for some bit of beauty one has given the world, is to take from death some of its sting.

Life has need of all the charm of word and sound, of color and carven stone that love can give it.

my *native city*

I.

A long walk. Tired and contented. I have been
   dreaming again.
My walk led me upon a hill to the southeast.

When at the top, I turned to see some cattle grazing
on the wayside—and behold! my native city lay
at my feet.

How silent, how small, how secluded! Like a new
toy in the grass, or a nest tucked away among the
trees of the surrounding valley; or—save for the
lines of smoke moving slowly to the north—like
a picture hanging in a gallery.

No one was near me, and only a few farmhouses in
the distance.

And I thought and dreamed of the wanderings of
men amid the toy-town in the grass,

Of the desires and hopes that had come and passed
in this nest among the trees.

I thought of my own wanderings, and remembered
some sleepless hours divine with the music of
the night.

A thousand memories filled me with the joys of
other years—memories of friends changed and
gone, and of the dawning sun lighting up the
nimble fancy worlds of youth.

I thought I could see the place where two lovers
met in the dim past, and out of the kiss of their

lips I crawled into the morning of the world—
and these poems after me.

Though I did not hear their words, unforgotten is
their lover's parley; for ere they knew me, it was I
who moved their lips to speech in the still night.

How much history has passed within this small
space of earth! Of no importance to the world;
yet all important the life of each to himself.

How many have lived and toiled and planned
here—how many, tired and careworn, have lain
down here to repose at night!

How many places where elegance and beauty once
reigned have fallen to bare uses! And how many,
merry with midnight music and the dance,
have been lifted into immortal joy, as if death
were not!

II.

O my native city! Thou knowest not how often I
have thought of thee when far away.

When I have wandered amid other scenes, and other
men and women and children have passed by me,
fondly have I thought of thee.

The cool shade of thy many trees, and the memory of
the gentle river at thy margin, have been a solace
to me in strange and distant places.
But thou wilt go on unconcerned as ever when I am
gone into the silent land.
Soon wilt thou forget that such a worm as I crawled
about thy streets in the shadow of thy buildings.
Within thy bosom I lay as a child, have grown to
manhood, and shall at last rest in dreamless sleep.
But thou, too, must pass away; and where now is
trade and manufacture God in his time will plant
another forest;
And it will grow, and no man will know that thou
dwelt there.
On newborn branches birds will whisper songs of
love, and flowered children of the wilderness
will drink the sun wine, and gloaming eve shall
know the wild dove's voice, and this race of
hurrying, contentious men shall lie—O so still
under the grass!
So, too, all things shall pass away—I, thou, country,
earth, solar systems.
What remains?—God!

to-morrow

How oft you've said to-morrow
Is time enough to speak a gentle word
To one whose olden friendship time had blurred
And set to naught sweet trysts of other years,
When life and love and faith were pledged with tears
That flowed as others' griefs you heard—
To-morrow you intend to speak the word.

'Mid discontent, to-morrow
Is then the golden day when you have thought
To build the temple which in dreams you'd wrought
So beautiful that aged men did say
With pride they knew you in their childhood's day.
Though old ambitions come to naught,
To-morrow is the golden time you've thought.

When worn with care, to-morrow
You'll change your course for one which steals away

To quiet lands where cooling shadows stray
And sunbeams tremble on the placid green,
Far off 'mid some forgotten olden scene;
And there as once you'll rest and play.
To-morrow you are going far away.

'Mid childhood scenes, to-morrow
With long embrace your heart will melt like snow,
Close by the Mother's heart whose love you know.
Those lips from which the rose is gone will press
Your joyous tearful cheek with mild caress.
Again you'll hear the cattle's low.
To-morrow you will kiss the brow of snow.

Art lonely? Then to-morrow
You'll freely yield your aching heart the time
To weave some love romance of purest rhyme.
With throbbing heart at fall of silent night
You'll speed to one who waits by evening light,
Where fancy love's sweet corals chime.
To-morrow you will yield your heart the time.

When age has come, to-morrow
You'll speak with God to leave some kindly deeds
Writ by your name that softened selfish creeds
Of man's slow moving love of brotherhood,
That brought new hope to them who near you stood
In life's dark streets or sunlit meads.
To-morrow you'll ask God for better deeds.

To-morrow, O to-morrow!
Fast fall the fading years. A thought, a dream
Of gentle words; of faith and love a theme;
A smile, a step or two, and then 'tis done.
Quick is the veering stream of life full run;
Yet in the crimson west still gleam
To-morrow and to-morrow's endless dream.

tell us,
philosopher

Philosopher, tell us what God is!

I can not. Man's mind is like a candle. God's mind is like all suns of the cosmos. We do but learn his formulas. Within the framework of matter and the laws of matter, may we endeavor to achieve some kind of life of the spirit: those mystical illuminated experiences, which in the humdrum of daily life seem so very unreal but which in exalted hours seem the only reality in a world of illusive values. I try to remember these exalted hours, to guide my steps through the lonely, unlighted way we all must travel.

Surely, this is what all religions mean when they speak of God in different tongues, and something philosophers mean when they speak of reality.

rest

The afternoon was cloudy, gusty, melancholy. The trees were dressed in their autumn splendor; the sycamores stripped to show their slender, silver bodies. I have lived long enough to have many friends in the cemetery. Here is the end, the last act, of that play which begins with so much promise; and which is attended in its progress by many, though petty, triumphs. To have come a long journey, to have done good work, to have been tired, and to have lain down here to rest, is, in the economy of the world, no matter for grief. Lord, "Help us to play the man."

eheu!

I was not called for greater tasks than these brief half-
    born songs;
I was not called to smite the lyre and right a
    nation's wrongs.
Not even was I bidden touch the fingertips of fame;
But in the eddies of a stream I scrolled my name.

Yet you who read perchance in after years by
    glow of light
In evening still, or by the music of some lonely stream,
Or on some silent, God-lit hill above the noisy world—
To you I whisper love, not fame, was my one dream.

Oh, that in youth but once I could have sung a
    song that held
The magic music of my soul, which ever upward welled
Against my tuneless lips! I sit alone and know the truth,
With broken harp beside the ashes of my youth.

thoughts on a september
night

The noise and litter of the day are gone. Out there—clear sky, bright stars, and silence.

A Great Mind seems to permeate the universe. We try to understand His thoughts, which are expressed in the beauty of the world and in the laws of nature. May we speak modestly when we speak of the laws of nature; we are still blind men blazing a trail with proofs and guesses.

We gave not ourselves this life. It came according to His plans, we know not how nor whence nor why.

Sometimes, in faith's luminous hours, we feel that the Great Mind is interested in our purposes and ideals.

When we are in danger, let us not expect to be saved by some sudden change in nature's laws; for this would make a great upheaval in the world, wrecking many innocent lives that depend upon nature's integrity.

In dark times, when life's turmoil is crushing us, instinctively we shall pray for help and courage.

Often man has made rules of conduct contrary to nature's modes; instead let us strive to obey nature's requirements for health of body and mind.

This is a beautiful world to look upon, which often leads us to think the Great Mind means well with us. But there is terrible evil in the world! May we be valiant against evil, in ourselves more than in others. May we not be overcome by the evil and sorrow of the world; for also there is virtue, well-being, happiness, and sometimes flashes of ecstasy.

We hope we will not be completely blotted out at the journey's end. We would continue in some manner to be with them we love. There is no proof, only a great hope.

The Great Mind may be trying to tell us many things; but we do not yet understand His language. No more can we tell the ant what we know of the stars. Though we seem vainly to question, we have hope that one day man will understand His language, and learn the purpose—if there is any—of man's sojourn on the earth.

When we consider the heavens (perhaps millions of galaxies and billions of inhabited planets) may we experience humility and reverence. We praise man's conquest of nature. Let us hope we soon will conquer human savagery and forever make an end of evil men provoking wars.

For some of us it is late afternoon, for some already it is the night. When the end comes, if there still remain some clear ray of consciousness, may we not be rebellious, remembering it is the time when the natural man, as if in sleep, must return to the elements. In that time may we feel the solace of them that journey home after their day of pleasant labor.

But if there be nothing else after the night has come, and the bright playlet of life in our brains is blotted out, yet would our speechless dust be thankful that once it throbbed with life and love on the beautiful earth.

Out there—clear sky, bright stars, and silence.